A Girl's Guide to Personal Hygiene

A Girl's Guide to Personal Hygiene

True Stories, Illustrated

Tallulah Pomeroy

SOFT SKULL

New York

A Girl's Guide to Personal Hygiene

First Soft Skull edition: 2018

Library of Congress Cataloging-in-Publication Data
Names: Pomeroy, Tallulah, author, illustrator.
Title: A girl's guide to personal hygiene: true stories, illustrated /
    by Tallulah Pomeroy.
Description: New York : Soft Skull, [2017]
Identifiers: LCCN 2017039573 | ISBN 9781593761820
    (pbk. : alk. paper) | ISBN 9781593761998 (ebook)
Subjects: LCSH: Girls—Health and hygiene—Comic books,
    strips, etc. | Graphic novels.
Classification: LCC RA 777.25 .P66 2017 | DDC 613/.04243—dc23
LC record available at https://lccn.loc.gov/2017039573

Cover design by www.salu.io
Book design by James Sutton

Published by Soft Skull Press
1140 Broadway, Suite 704
New York, NY 10001
www.softskull.com

Soft Skull titles are distributed to the trade by Publishers Group West
Phone: 866-400-5351

Printed in Canada
10 9 8 7 6 5 4 3 2 1

This book is dedicated to the girl who did a shit in the sink. You're an inspiration to many.

CONTENTS

FOREWORD

A Girl's Guide to Personal Hygiene began when I over-heard two girls talking about a friend of theirs. When this friend had been on tour with the rugby team at her university, she'd drunkenly "done a shit in the sink." "Ew, gross," said one of the girls to the other. "She's not a girl if she did that. She may have a vagina, but she's not a girl." I thought that was pretty funny. I wondered how many things I had done that would make me not a girl in their eyes. And what about my girlfriends? I set up a Facebook group to find out what disgusting things everyone had done, intending to make a small book out of the stories. It wasn't just nosiness. I'd realized that most of the pressure to behave in a certain feminine way comes from other women. If we could admit that we are pretty gross—though not all of us have gone as far as that rugby player—maybe we could relax a little.

But the seeds of the project were sown earlier, with *Wetlands* by Charlotte Roche. "Read this," said a friend. "It'll make you feel like a prude." I did; it did. In the novel, the protagonist, Helen, is stuck in the hospital following some anal pube–trimming gone wrong, and if that makes you squirm, just you wait. Helen unabashedly revels in all her crevices and odors. I'd rarely even heard anyone say "discharge," and here was Helen joyfully wiping hers in public places for the pleasure of knowing it would get on someone's hands. It was a revelation. It didn't make me want to go smearing my bodily fluids out in the world, but I became aware of things I do that I keep secret for fear of being improper. I'd been indoctrinated into being uncomfortable with my own body. We're told to take care of our "lady gardens" with a delicate "intimate wash," destroying all our lovely self-cleaning systems in the process, and—as Helen would say—getting rid of the attractive personal wafts that tingle the nostrils of admirers. Girls who think we should smell floral, I decided, aren't having much fun.

The response to the Facebook group was amazing. At first we were tentative, but soon it turned into this huge repulsive outpouring. I almost wished I could close the lid again. There were stories that made defecating in a sink seem like a pretty polite thing to do. *Where's your modesty, girls?* went a voice in my head, probably the voice of the teacher who told my date at the school disco to take his hands off my bum. *Sure*, the voice went, *we're all human, but do we need to shout about it?* And while I admired people's honesty, it was another thing for it to be my own project. I'd meet friends of friends who knew of the group, and they'd start going into detail about the last time they shat themselves in public. *Nice to meet you, too*, I'd think, *but we're at the pub. Can I drink my beer and not talk about poo for a minute?* Just because I started this damn thing doesn't mean I'm hungry for poo stories. I'm not making this book to fill a gap in my bookshelf, because nobody was writing about my favorite topic, personal hygiene.

I have a tendency to birth ideas and then abandon them. Like the goat farm I was going to set up with my sister. We made a list of appropriate goat names, from Abigail to Priscilla, and that was where it ended. No doubt the *Girl's Guide* would have gone the same way if it weren't for the collective enthusiasm of the other girls who were taking part. They gave me confidence, and I didn't want to let them down. I'd been made uncomfortable in my new position as a receptacle for other people's dirty stories, but it was exactly that sense of shame I wanted to combat. I began to like the new conversations we were having in the pub about what made women feminine and what an equivalent book would be for men. And the group evolved on its own, becoming something more than just an outlet for long-buried atrocities. We started asking questions— "PLEASE, IS IT JUST ME?!!!"—and offering helpful hints about things like those new period pants I've yet to try.

The responsibility I felt toward the other girls was also a burden. What had begun as a tiny idea was becoming unwieldy and public and a little bit scary. I enlisted the help of my friend James, a graphic designer. We'd wanted to make a book together for a while, but due to the aforementioned habit of carelessly ditching ideas, I'd never managed to give him any material. Now I needed him to relieve some of the pressure on me and provide another perspective. James is a very clean person, as many designers tend to be, and his enthusiasm reassured me I wasn't making something so obscene I'd be hounded from society. We chose which stories to publish together, gravitating toward habits and private routines over anecdotes. Accidents happen to us all; no surprises there. I wanted to hear the things girls do but usually hide from everyone, even in our climate of public sharing. It was interesting to see which stories we each found unendurable. James was made faint by the one about freely bleeding into your pants, which didn't bother me at all. I was more disturbed by people eating their own toenails. James made sure we chose stories of varying length and tone, while I looked out for ones that would make good illustrations.

Starting the drawings was a whole new kettle of fish. Originally I'd envisioned little cartoons, drawn over the course of one afternoon. But now that people were paying attention, that didn't feel appropriate. Women had taken time to write their confessions in funny and interesting ways; I wanted my drawings to live up to the stories. After the usual procrastination period of several months, I started laboring over sticky pen-and-ink drawings and meticulous collages, trying to be "professional." The *Girl's Guide* was never meant to be professional, though, and it was when I returned to what I love best—drawing quickly and easily with my fountain pen, no drafts or second thoughts—that it came together. It's funny how long it takes to learn that what comes naturally is the good stuff.

The first incarnation of the project was a small zine with twenty illustrated stories, risograph-printed by Hato Press in London. We launched it with an exhibition at a youth center in Bristol in the U.K. I hoped teenagers would read the stories and learn early on that girls can be gross, and that's all right. Get 'em while they're young. It's probably too late for my grandmother; she came to the launch, beautifully dressed for the occasion, but I'm sadly never going to hear the word "discharge" pass her lips. My favorite response to the show was from an eighteen-year-old boy: "It's such a relief. I'm moving in with three girls next year, and now I know they're human, too."

Now the book is much longer and fuller than the original zine, and I'm interested to see how the *Girl's Guide* fares with a new audience. It's one thing to have interest and support from like-minded girls in England, with our history of toilet humor, but will it cross the pond? That remains to be seen. The stories in this book are honest and open reports but from only a tiny subset of women. I wanted us to feel comfortable sharing and talking online, so I kept the group private: No boys allowed! This let the conversation be free and gave a sense of solidarity, as if we belonged to a special club of women. But it also shut the group off to women outside my limited social circle. This edition of the book gained a broader range once we enabled anonymous submissions, but it's still a much narrower representation than it could be.

We still use the Facebook group, sharing the joys of snot bubbles and the woes of the copper coil, and I've been rendered fairly unshockable. I'm hairy all over, and have quite a distant relationship with deodorant, but I feel more feminine than ever, and no longer at odds with my own body. Maybe you'll feel that too, after reading. Or maybe you'll just have a laugh. I hope you enjoy the helpful hints enclosed in these pages, and if we meet at a party, feel free to unburden yourself of your most recent poo story.

TALLULAH POMEROY

HAIR

I sometimes use my hair to floss between my teeth.

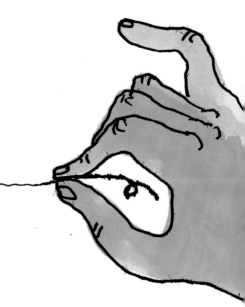

I only shave my ankles, so it looks like I'm wearing fluffy trousers. Hehe.

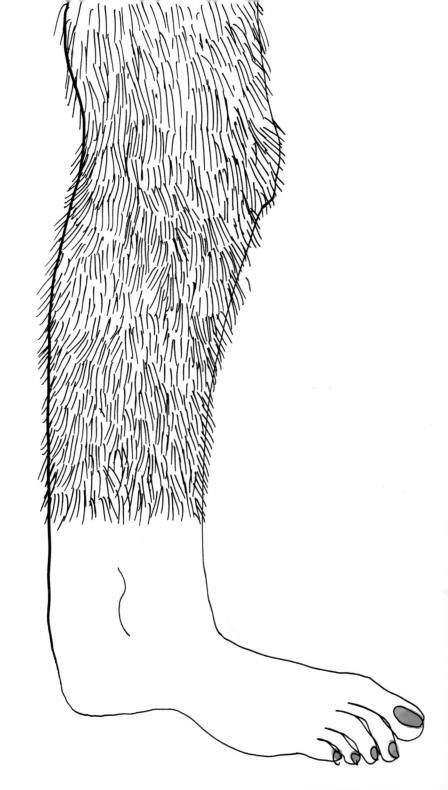

I religiously use my pubes as a kind of loofah when I'm in the shower. I get the soap all cappuccino-foamy on my woopsie and then use the suds to wash the rest of my body.

Sometimes in the shower when I remove the hair that's collected in my butt crack, I put it on the shower wall and make it into a picture. One time I created this really abstract masterpiece inspired by Picasso.

When I got my first pube, I was so proud. I pulled it out, wrapped it in a tissue, and kept it in a little wooden box on my shelf for four years.

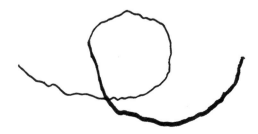

Any gals with PCOS (polycystic ovary syndrome) in the house? I have always been super hairy. The older and more cysty I get, the more hairy I become, so now I have dark pubey hair down ma thighs and round ma bum. I get the excess waxed off when I wanna feel fancy, and the last wax I got, I was talking to the lady about it, and she looked me dead in the eyes while ripping the hair out of me and said, "It's hard for you; you have man hair."

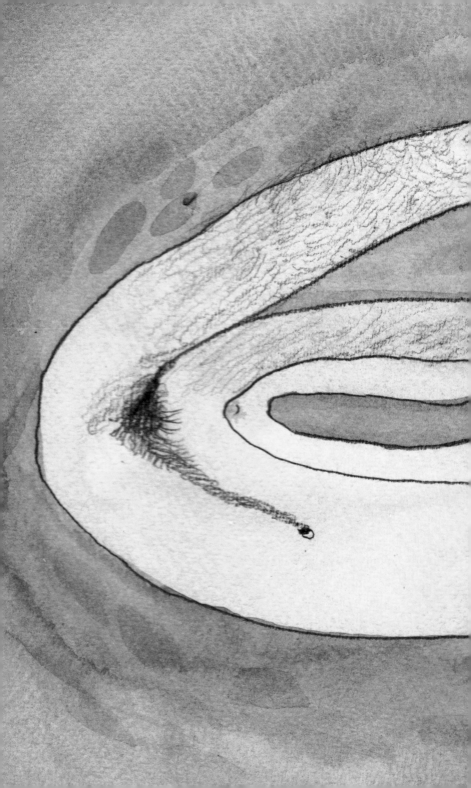

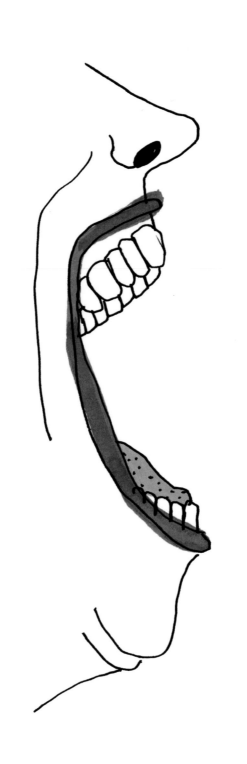

Sometimes I trim my armpit hair over the sink and it goes on my toothbrush, which is also lying on the sink's rim and already has a little pea of toothpaste on it, and then it sticks on the toothbrush, but one time I had run out of toothpaste and it had been a big effort to squeeze some out, so I just brushed my teeth with the hair glued onto the toothpaste.

Lying in bed,
I pick out
my bum hairs.
Very satisfying.

The texture of my gray pubes is different from the dark ones, all ridged and curly, and in bed at night I like feeling the hairs. Often I pull one out and run it between my fingers, enjoying the little lumps and bumps.

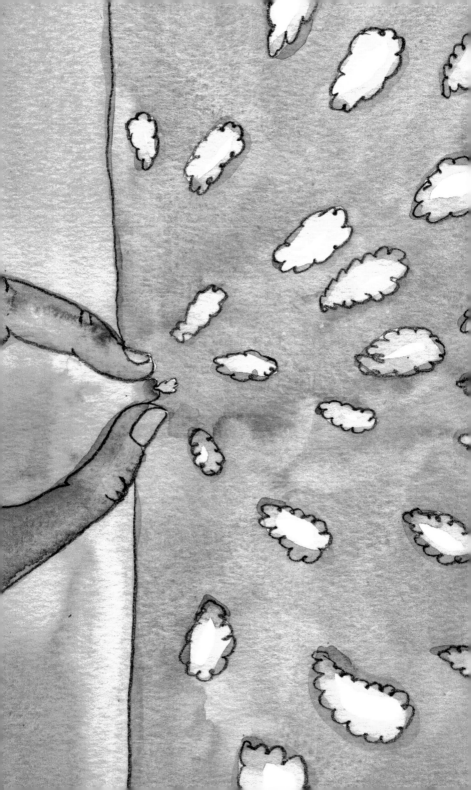

I scoop out my earwax with my long acrylic nails and then hide it places.

I pick the inside of the tops of my ears. Little scabs form. I wish I didn't.

One of my childhood friends was so much "girlier" than I was. I sometimes envied it and tried to emulate it. In our teens, her wardrobe became designer and her body waxed. She would relentlessly flirt with boys as she played up her ditziness, and they loved it. I didn't get attention like that—I didn't feel girly. One morning after sleeping over, I woke up in her bed on the side next to the wall. As I shifted into consciousness, I noticed a MASSIVE booger collection (MBC!) between the mattress and the wall! It was shocking and exciting, and I absolutely loved it! My idea of femininity started to change right then and there.

Something I really love about my shower routine is getting really nice and dry, laying my towel on the floor, sitting on it with my legs bent, crouching over to have a good search for any ingrown hairs around my lady bits, and fishing them out with a needle. It also means I can find any spots that need squeezing, which are rarer but more exciting. I found an enormous spot once on my inner thigh right near the crease where leg turns into vagina. It was so perfect: a big, hard, massive white head. I squeezed it and heard an actual pop, and some of it went on my face because I was leaned in so close. It was frustrating not being able to share such a moment with anyone who really understood.

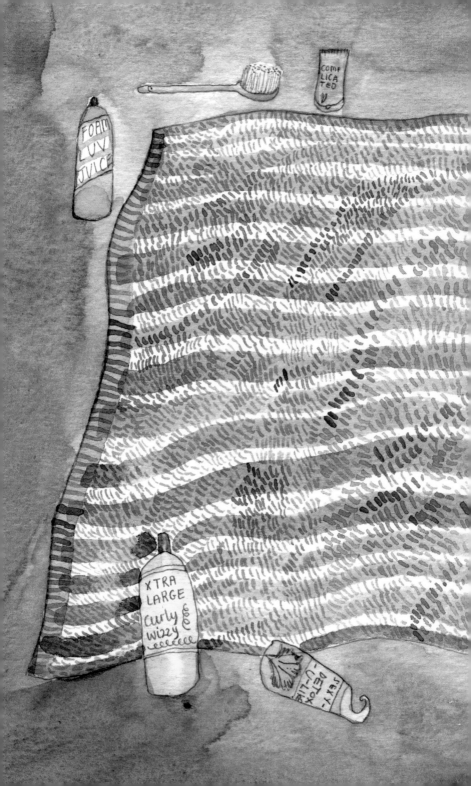

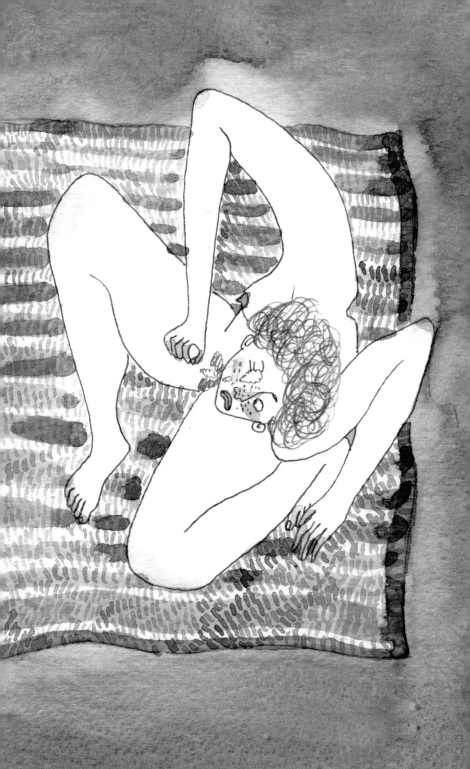

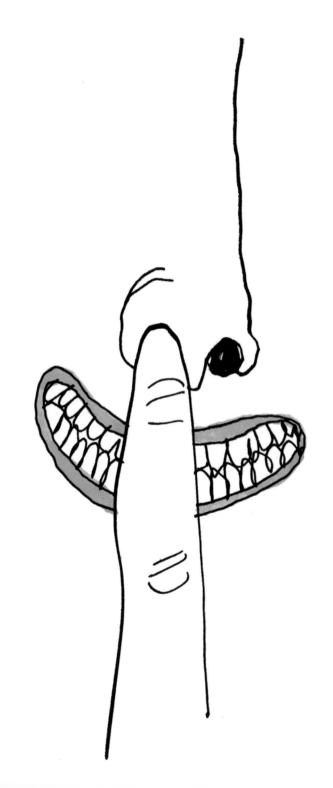

I sometimes like to pick my nose while I masturbate. It helps.

I have an enlarged tonsil. This enlarged tonsil has craters in it, not unlike the moon, except fleshier, of course. Every once in a while, if I start to feel something back in there, I use a Q-tip to push on my enlarged tonsil. Gnarled off-white balls called tonsil stones pop out of the fleshy craters. Sometimes I gag because, well, I'm sticking Q-tips down my throat. Also, the tonsil stones smell horrible. It's completely disgusting and wonderfully satisfying.

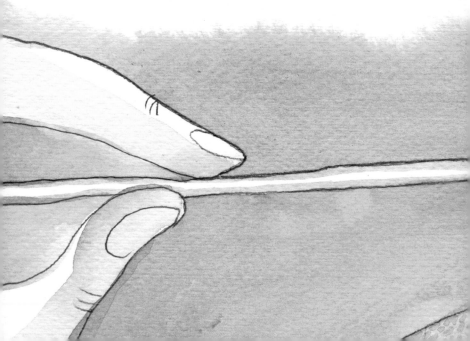

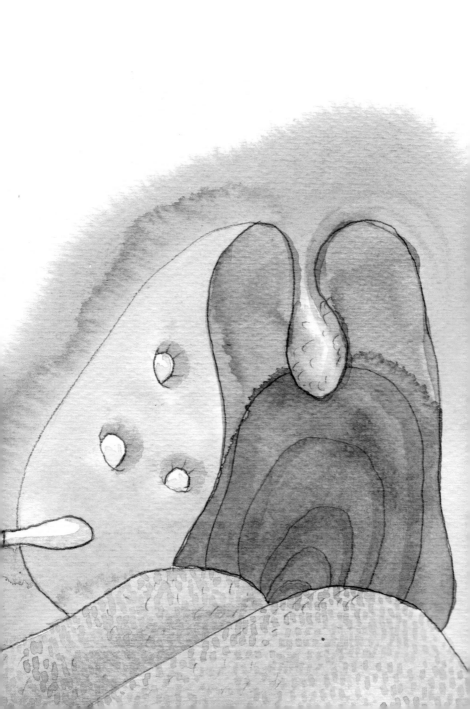

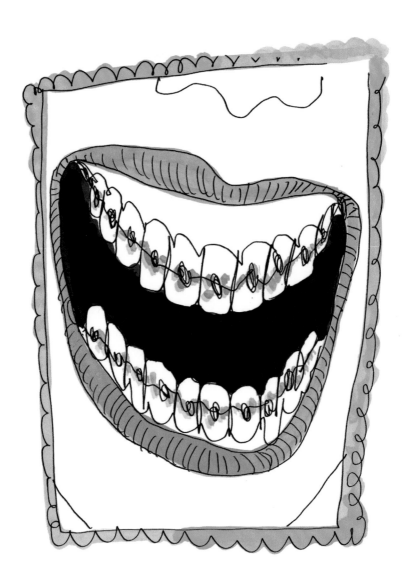

I used to have a couple of medals hanging off my mirror. When I had braces, I would pick the grime out of my braces and wipe it on the straps of these medals. There was a lot of grime there. I called it my "museum."

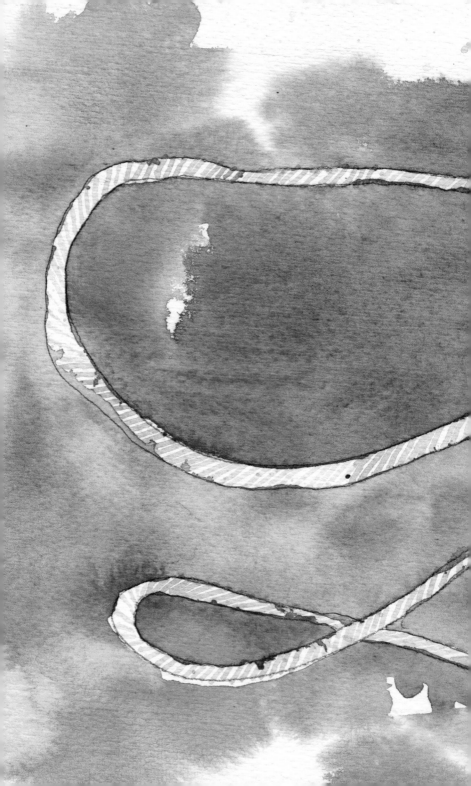

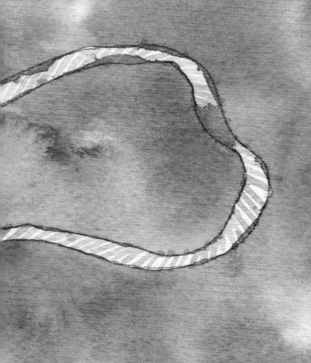

After twelve years of periods, I still have trouble with not leaking on fresh white sheets, which is especially unladylike when you're a guest. So a couple of years ago I came up with this neat trick where I roll up a square of loo roll and stick it in between my butt cheeks. Works so well I feel like it should be a marketed product. *Stuff ya cheeks, save ya sheets!*

Sometimes I'll just let myself bleed rather than use a cup or tampon. I'm running out of pants!

As a young girl, I came across my auntie's sanitary towels on the windowsill, but being young and oblivious, I concluded that they were waxing strips and put two on each leg. I couldn't understand why they didn't work and just kept them on my legs all day walking around with them under my tracksuit bottoms. They all fell off and out of my trackies as I was walking around town.

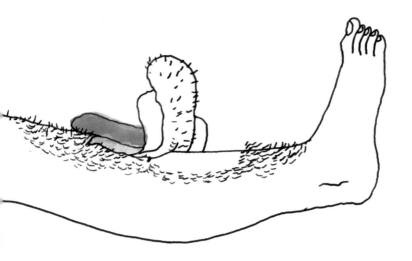

When I was camping, I emptied my Mooncup into a shallow part at the edge of a river. For a while I sat and watched little fish nibble on bits of my womb. I had lots of profound thoughts about the "circle of life."

I like to smell the contents of my Mooncup because someone once told me theirs smelled like beef. Mine has never smelled meaty. It's far sweeter, like a Parma Violet. Does each woman have her own menstrual scent?

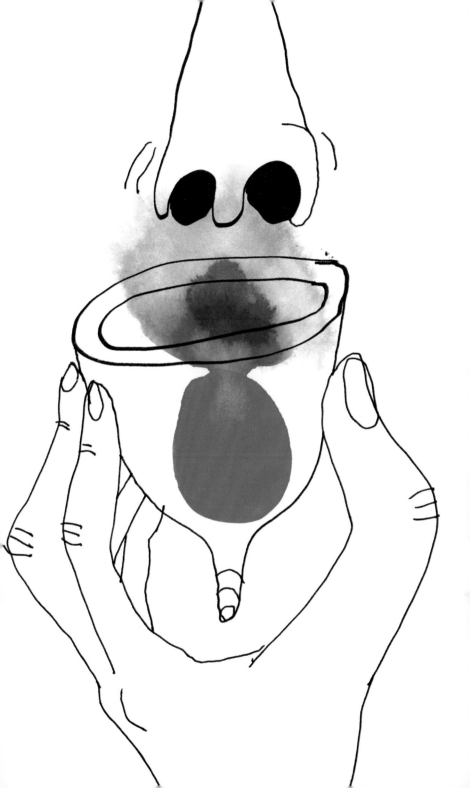

Once, on Christmas Day with my dad's fam, I came on my period early. I hadn't thought to bring any sannies, and I'd never used a tampon. I rooted round in the bathroom and was only able to find tampons (not even with applicators—I was really in the lurch), so I just put it SOMEWHERE near my vagina (I don't to this day know where I managed to wedge it) and continued with my day. Later we were playing a round of Balderdash in my auntie's pristine living room, and I was in my new white PJs on the new cream sofa. Halfway through, I felt a leakage and whispered to my sis to check when I stood up. I stood up and sat down real quick, and she was like, "Yep, yep, there is a situation." So I ran to the loo, and she covered the twenty-centimeter patch of blood with her jumper (bless her soul). She told my auntie, who swiftly came over and flipped the sofa cushion, SOMEHOW leaving everyone none the wiser until my mum, two sisters, and dad came into the bathroom to check if I'm all right while I was rinsing my bloody pajamas in the bath.

NOOKS

&

CRANNIES

I like smelling my knickers when I'm sat on the toilet. Mainly because every time I get thrush or something, the doctor asks me if my discharge smells strange. So if I'm always checking, I'll know when something's up. Clever me.

I remember being a kid and masturbating in the backseat of the car with my parents up front and sister in the car seat. I don't think I have a fetish for masturbating out in the world, but I've definitely rubbed out a quickie in the bathroom at work and then immediately gone back to the bar customers. Probably I washed my hands?

How about that great feeling of a fart rolling between your fanny lips?

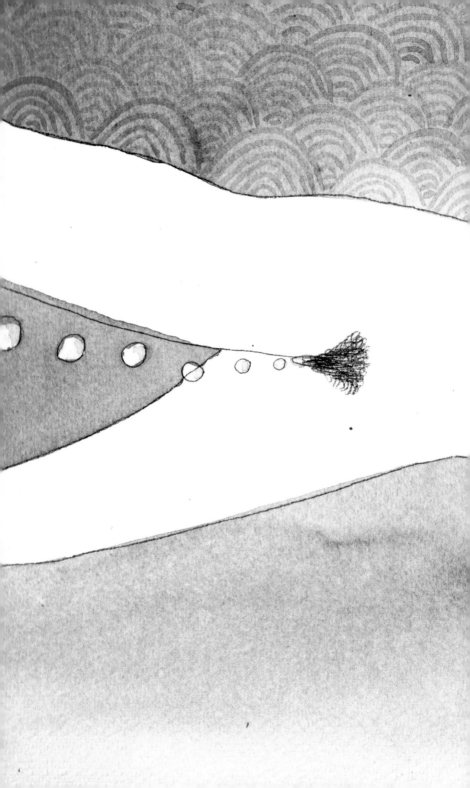

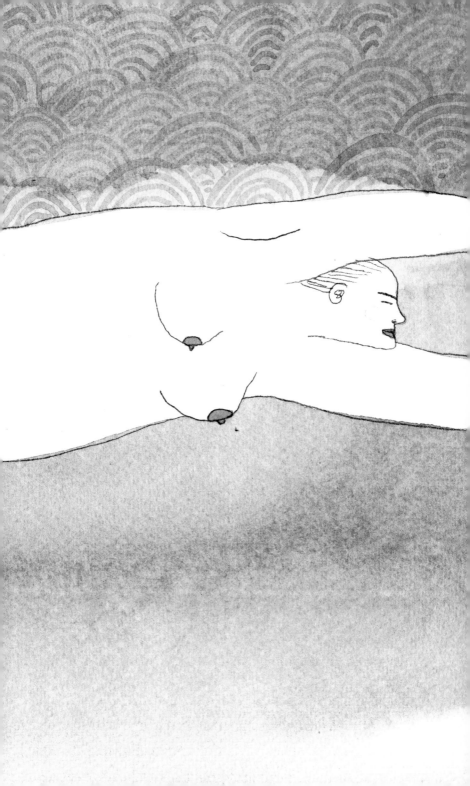

After wearing undies all day, sometimes my pubes can get crusted up with some of that discharge. So I just go ahead and pick that off at the end of the day.

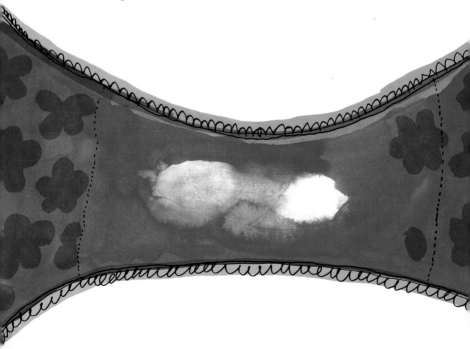

I recently had a particularly stubborn case of bacterial vaginosis. It was bad timing—I'd met someone new and we'd started sleeping together, and all of a sudden I smelled like the bottom of a bin. I explained about my "delicate ecosystem," but a course of antibiotics failed to clear it up. One day, sad and smelly, I sat on the loo and felt something coming out of my body. My first thought was PROLAPSE! because this is one of my deepest fears. But when I reached inside, I felt not my internal organs but the source of my BV: a slimy old tampon. My period had finished two weeks before.

When I held it up to inspect, I felt that mixture of horror and pride we feel when something appalling comes out of our own body.

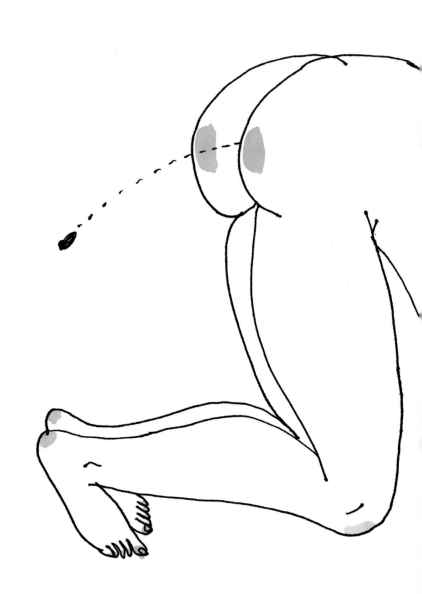

I quite often get trapped wind, and I find the best method to ease it out is to go into the bathroom, put my bare bum in the air, and wriggle it about a bit. Once, I did this, and on releasing a fabulous fart, I looked down and saw a tiny pea-size poo on the floor. I think I was a bit drunk. I just remember laughing at it for ages before I picked it up with loo roll.

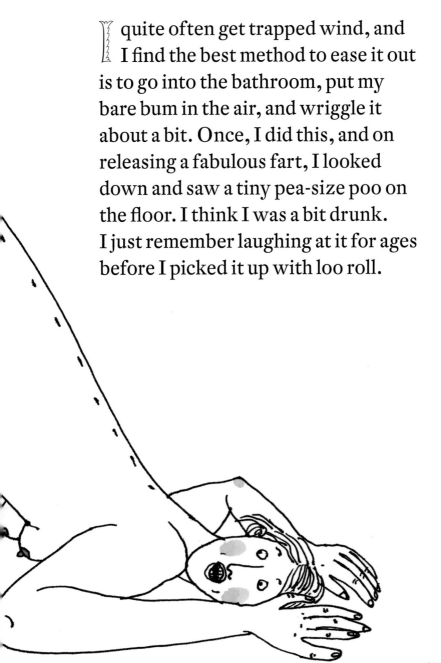

When I am in a public toilet and need to do a fart but don't want anyone to hear me, I pull my bum cheeks wide apart so the fart can just slip out breezily without any noise at all!

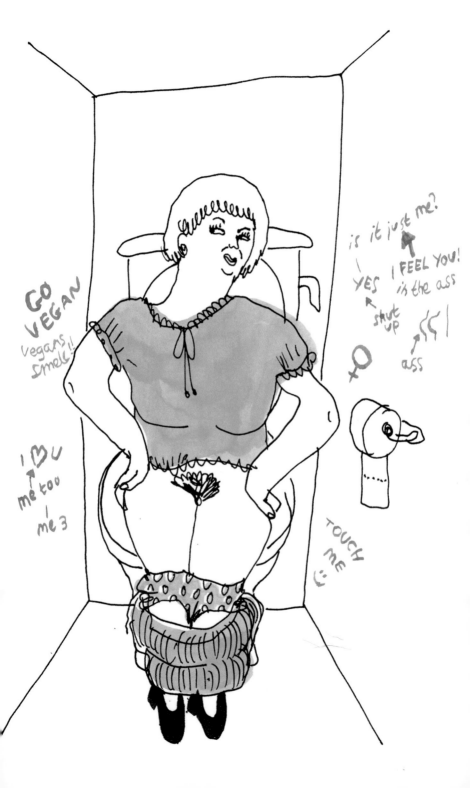

When I was a teenager and sitting at the family computer in the kitchen, I had a thought: "What would happen if I just shit my pants right here? Like, how would it feel?" And as I sat, probably on instant messenger, I just let it all out. Turns out it feels exactly how one would imagine.

I was at a boy's house and I was a bit drunk, and suddenly and desperately I needed the loo. I sat down and let it all come out with a sigh, and before I knew it (and much to my delight), a big ol' poo was on its way, too. Then I looked to my right, and there was the toilet. Much to my surprise, I wasn't sat on the toilet at all. I was sat on a bidet. I laughed and laughed and laughed and cleared up my poo, which wasn't pleasant, and then went back in and pretended everything was all gravy. I was smiling inside for the rest of the evening.

My house doesn't have an inside toilet, so I have a jug that I pee in every night and sometimes in the morning. I pour it on some plants and leave it to dry during the day. When I'm on my period it's red pee, which is fun.

Isn't it kinda gross when you have a poo and go to wipe your bottom but you have lots of discharge so your loo roll just slides out of control all up your crack with a nice dischargey-pooey mix? Yum yum.

S ometimes if I'm pooping in a rush, I push on my gooch area from inside my vagina, and it pops right out.

When I've spent the energy fixing myself a nice hot bubble bath at the end of the day, I can't be bothered to leave the tub just because I have to pee, so I relieve myself in the bath. How bad could a little bit of urine in a big tub of water be, anyway?

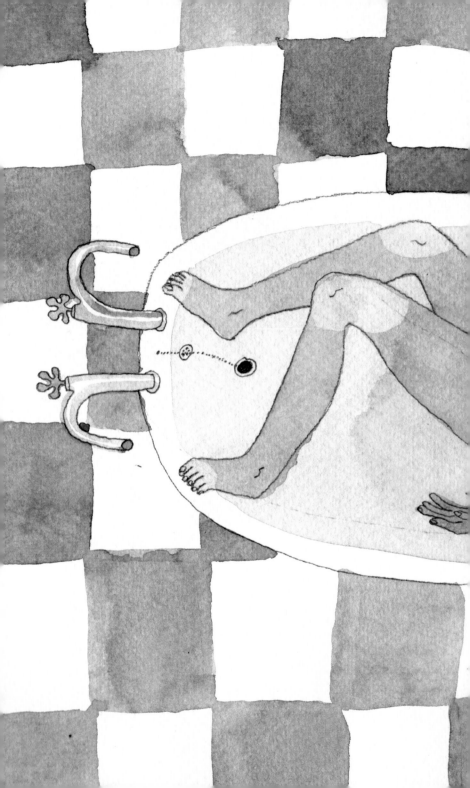

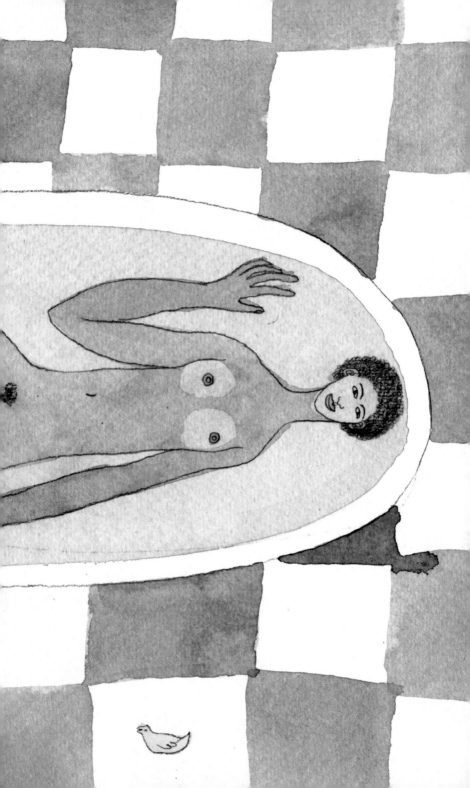

L oads of women shit when giving birth. (I mean, you gotta push really hard.) Sometimes they give the dad-to-be a little net to fish the poops out of the birthing pool.

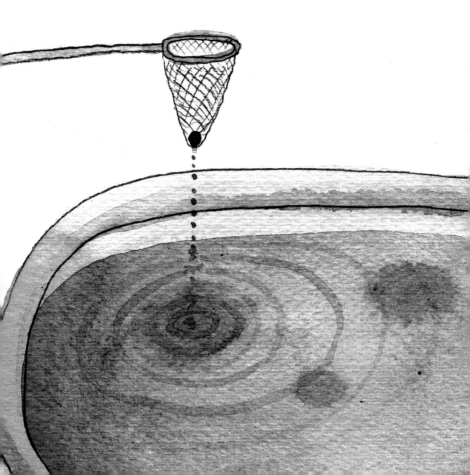

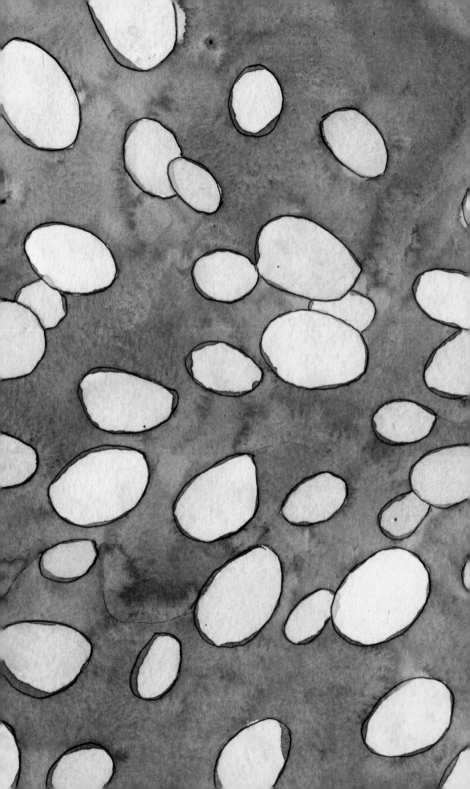

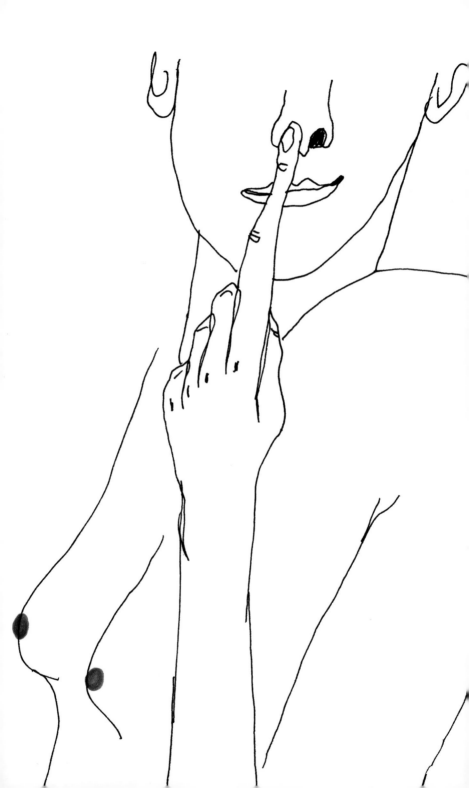

I have an abnormally deep belly button, and when you put your finger in it and smell, it smells like rotten fish. Sometimes I get people to put their fingers in it, too, just to see their reactions. I try to clean it when I remember, but I'm quite fond of it, and I reckon I check on it at least once a day.

I maintain my flexibility with the specific intention of being able to keep on biting my own toenails into old age.

I eat my sleep. You know, that yellowy sometimes crispy, sometimes gooey eye stuff that you normally have in the morning. I like the taste of it. Sometimes I don't notice I'm doing it in front of people. Nobody's ever said anything, though, so maybe it's not that gross?

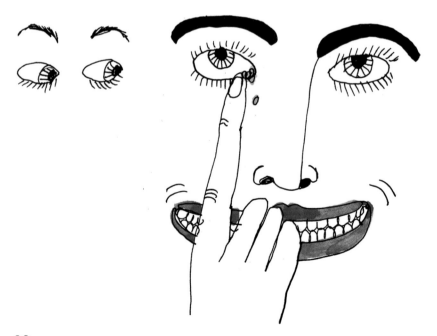

My boyfriend once found an old dried-up grain of rice in my belly button. Couldn't remember the last time I had had rice.

One New Year's, when about to have a three-way, I somehow decided the best way to deal with my bloody tampon was to put it in the teapot full of water next to the love-bed. I then left said teapot in the bathroom for my boyfriend's mum to discover and freak the fuck out about. I painted her a new teapot in apology, but I don't think she's used it.

Eating boogers is salty and delicious. They often have nice textures as well.

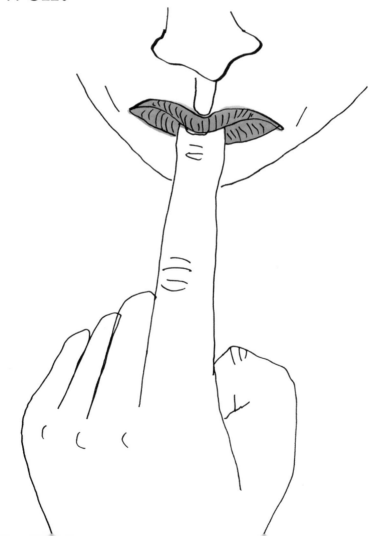

I'll often put a finger down in my underwear to see if my period's leaking, and after, if a little blood is on it, instead of washing my hands I'll just put the finger in my mouth.

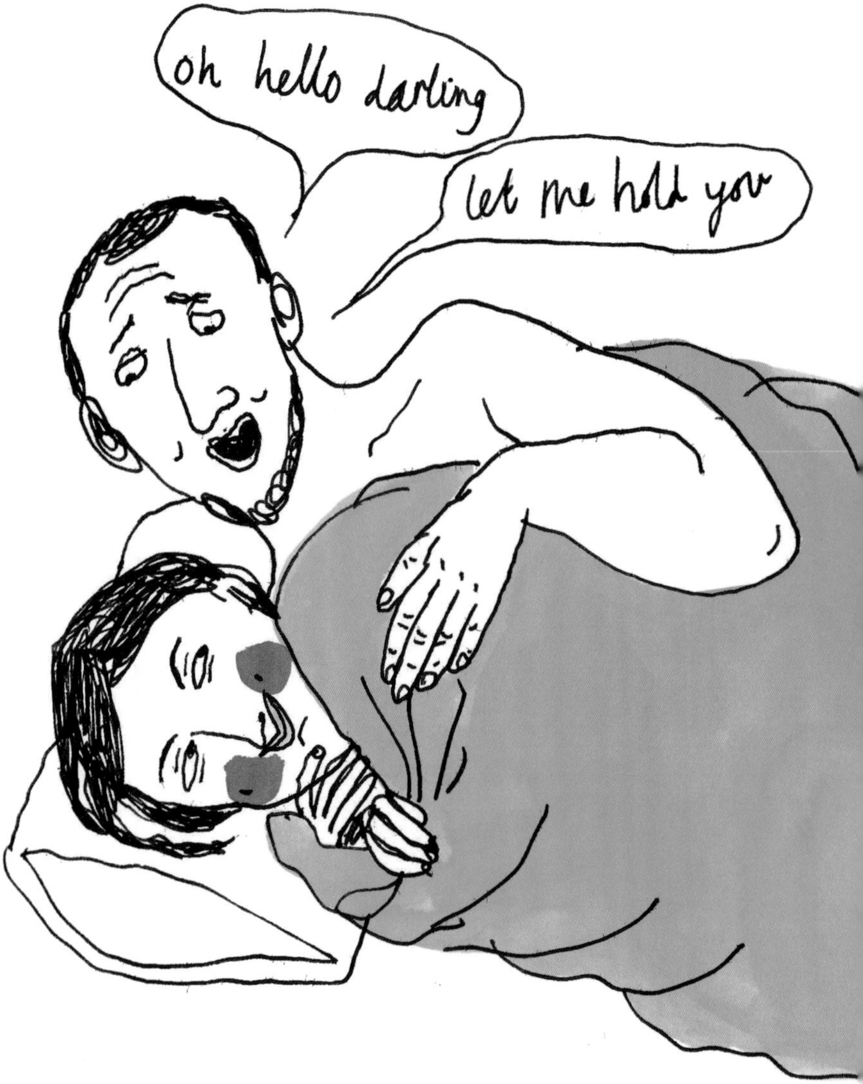
oh hello darling
let me hold you

Sometimes I hold my farts so that when bae gets into bed and spoons me, I can fart on him.

My amore and I once spent a happy afternoon shaving each other's pubes with his new razor. I shaved his bum crack, and he was so unfamiliar with the sensation of smooth bum cheeks rubbing together that he thought he'd pooed himself.

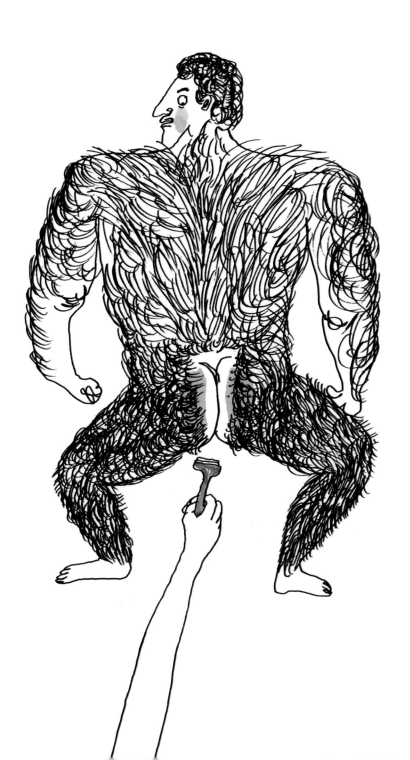

To avoid ruining the moment by going to the loo, I like to subtly whip my tampon out just before sex. Pretty sure nobody notices. Not until they clean under their bed, anyway.

A cum blanket is a necessary item. My bed is up a ladder, and I cannot be bothered to walk down it and then sit on the toilet for twenty minutes waiting for it to slowly "cum" out. Neither do I want to lie in it all night feeling like I am weeing myself. So I like to wrap the blanket around me like a massive nappy and sleep aaaaall night long. It's very comforting.

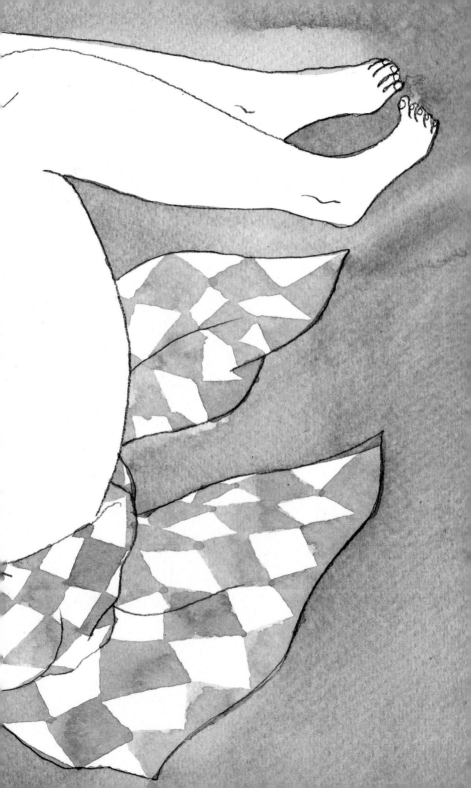

ACKNOWLEDGMENTS

Many thanks to Yuka for her excitement about this project; it's been encouraging and galvanizing to work on this with you. Thanks to James for so willingly immersing himself in feminine hygiene. And a really big thanks to all the girls who contributed to the group in the first place: your openness and humor have been wonderful! This wouldn't exist without you.